The One True Gospel

For the only Way of Salvation

Frederick Serjeant

Showing from the Bible how to distinguish between the one true gospel and those that are false

DEDICATION

I dedicate this book to my very dear wife Mary who has been my constant companion, support and encouragement for over 60 years.

Table of Contents

END NOTES page 79

Introduction

Right from the start, I want you to know that in this little book I am not going to try to sell you something. If you read on, my hope is that you will discover here an absolutely free gift awaiting you that is the most wonderful, fantastic, tremendous, marvellous gift anyone could possibly desire. Am I exaggerating, like some dubious used-car salesman?

A car salesman is out to make a profit. This is about an absolutely free gift from God, it is all of God's *grace*!ⁱ You cannot earn this gift, you can only receive it.

But let me make it clear - I would be less than honest with you if I failed to warn you that this gift is not given to all. In fact, it is only given to a minority. It would seem that the vast majority go through life heedless of this precious gift.

As I trust to show, this gift comes to us wrapped up in what is known as the 'Gospel of Jesus Christ'.

With that as my main purpose, allow me to explain that this little book has also been written because there are those who "peddle false gospels" [ii] in our day, by which many have been deceived. This will become clearer as we go on.

A Simple Gospel?

In presenting teachings such as these, many a teacher or preacher will find himself confronted by some who regard themselves as Christians – sometimes those of long standing-who cry, "We want just a **simple Gospel!**"

Well, in essence the gospel can be presented in a simple way, but all that it implies, is far from simple. Otherwise, we would not need all the books of the New Testament!

The Gospel may be simply expressed, but it is not simplistic. Sadly, there are those who seem to be unwilling to accept the apostle Paul's instruction to his assistant in the work of the gospel, Timothy:

"Study to present yourself approved by God, a workman who needs not be ashamed, rightly handling the word of truth."   *2* Timothy 2:15

We must be prepared to do some real thinking if we are to understand what the Scriptures teach about the Gospel.

Our Aim

We spell out our aim as follows:

1. To show how someone who is new to the Christian Faith may discover what the teaching of Jesus and his apostles is, concerning the way a person is saved. That is, how he or she is rescued from all that cuts him or her[iii] [see Page 79] off from God - both now and in eternity.

2. To show that the 'Gospel' is the message that opens the Way of Salvation.

3. To show that there is only ONE true Gospel but numerous false ones.

4. To encourage all who may already call themselves 'Christians' to examine themselves to see whether they are truly in the Way of Salvation. - Asking two key questions:

(a) For whom did Christ die?

(b) What is your part in getting saved?

5. To encourage all who believe the true Gospel to take their part in fulfilling the "Great Commission" of Jesus. (see Matthew 28:18 – 20)

It has been written as much for beginners as for those who have seen themselves as Christians for many years. I have tried to avoid using 'theological jargon', but every kind of study has its special vocabulary and this is no exception. However, I hope to explain any special word in the text or in a footnote. Direct quotations from the Bible will usually be in **italics** *like this.*

HYMNS

At the end of each Chapter I shall be including the words of a 'Hymn' – a Christian song. Some were written many years ago. I have included them to illustrate the teaching and to give a pause for thought. I hope you will meditate on the words of the Hymns. If you are interested, tunes for them can usually be found on the Internet.

Chapter 1

Do You Have a Problem?

It is possible that we start with a problem - or what may thought to be a problem. This concerns your present ideas about the Bible!

It may be that you already have some knowledge of the Bible, or that all your thoughts about it have come to you 'second-hand'. If we are to continue our journey of discovery together, I am going to ask you to suspend your present attitudes and assumptions for the time being. I trust you will be able to come to a better or fuller view as we proceed.

The reason I suggest this, is because all the content that follows will simply be applied teaching from the Bible and, I trust, will be fully in accord with all that is revealed in the Bible.

It will be most helpful then, if you get hold of a Bible as soon as you can so that you can look up the 'references' (quotations) and read them in their **contexts.** There are many versions of the Bible in English. Some are   better for our purposes   than   others.   So   I   will   be recommending those in Appendix A at the back of the book.

"Context is King!"

What do I mean by that? I mean that it is all too easy to take what people say out of context, so that the meaning is distorted. So it is with the Bible. Some short passages (verses) if isolated from their contexts can be misunderstood or made to mean something false. Many of the errors that have crept into Christian teachings have arisen through this practice. This why I say 'Context' must be king! In other words, the wider context must rule –

govern - the meaning or understanding of the shorter text.

To explain to those who are new to the Bible - the Bible has conveniently been divided into Books, Chapters and numbered 'verses'. The most famous verse in the Bible is 'John 3:16. That indicates it is found in the book called John's Gospel, Chapter three and verse sixteen. If you look it up now you will find it begins with the words "*God so loved the world ....*". This verse of Scripture is widely known and widely quoted. But it needs to be understood in the context of the paragraph in which it stands, and then in the Chapter, then in the context of John's Gospel. That in turn is to be understood within the whole New Testament section and lastly in the context of the whole Bible! Of course, newcomers to these things will not yet know much about the wider context. But all can begin by reading the immediate contexts. At the very least let **that** rule our understanding.

If many who see themselves as Christians actually studied the context of John 3: 16 for example, they may come to understand it in a very different way from their present understanding. But we shall have more to say about that later.

All who have a reasonable knowledge of the Bible's content will know that the Bible consists of two sections named the Old Testament and the New Testament. (O.T. and N.T.) The O.T. Contains 39 books that give an account of God's dealing with mankind - and especially with the Jewish nation before Christ came into the world. The N.T. Contains 27 books that relate to God's dealing with mankind since Jesus came. So then, the Bible is not just one Book, but 66 books! Some books are Narrative and Historical. Others are Prophetic. (contain prophecies). Others are Poetry. In most books there is an overlap of the forms.

The word **'Gospel'** comes from the old English "God's spel" meaning God's speech or story.

But it is not a very good translation of the original Greek word. (The original N.T. was written in common Greek and the O.T in Hebrew.) The original Greek word using English letters, is '*euangellion*' and it simply means 'good news'. It refers to the good news concerning God's kingdom and our salvation through Jesus Christ.

That Good News is what this book is all about. In the New Testament there are four books called 'Gospels' - according to Matthew, Mark, Luke and John. These give an account of what Jesus did and taught until he returned to heaven. If you are not familiar with these Four Gospels, I suggest you start reading them as you study this book.

You will quickly discover as you begin to read, that John the Baptist was sent as a prophet to prepare the way for the coming of the Christ[iv]. He had one simple message: "*Repent and believe the gospel!*" Christ himself began his ministry with the same message, "*Repent and believe the gospel!*" (see Mark 1:4 and 1:15)

As we shall see, the Good News is made known to us through the 'double door' of **repentance** and **faith.**[v]

All the books of the Bible were divinely inspired. The one book in the N.T. that was written particularly to explain and apply the Gospel, is the one written by the apostle Paul to Christians at Rome – named 'The Epistle (or Letter) to the Romans'. Be warned! It is not easy reading for newcomers.

The whole New Testament, refers to the Gospel and we shall be showing this, but we shall frequently be referring to Paul's Letter. 'Romans' is found immediately following the Four Gospels and The Acts of the Apostles. So let's make a start!

HYMN

Almighty God, your Word is cast
Like seed into the ground;
Now let the dew of heaven descend
And righteous fruits abound.

Let not the foe of Christ and man
This holy seed remove,
But give it root in every heart
To bring forth fruits of love.

Let not the world's deceitful cares
The rising plant destroy,
But let it yield a hundred fold
The fruits of peace and joy.

Oft as the precious seed is sown,
Your quickening grace bestow
That all whose souls the truth receive
Its saving power may know.

By John Cawood 1775-1852

Chapter 2

The Need of Salvation

Humanity's Desperate Predicament

The Apostle[vi] Paul in writing to the saints [vii] in Rome after the opening greetings make a statement that indicates his purpose in writing to them:

" For I am not ashamed of the gospel, for it is the power of God for salvation to everyone who believes, to the Jew first and also to the Greek. [viii] *For in it the righteousness of God is revealed from faith for faith, as it is written, "The righteous shall live by fai*th." Romans 1:16-17

This is a key statement which Paul goes on to explain and apply. He begins as we shall do, with man's desperate predicament. When I refer to *man* or *men*, I am meaning the human race, including females as well as males, children as well as adults.

All men by nature are in an awful state, whether they realise it or not. We have all come into this world spiritually dead towards God.

(see Ephesians 2:1,5 Colossians 2:13)

To use another picture, you were born into this world spiritually deaf and blind. So all are totally corrupted by sin. In using the word 'totally', we mean affected in **every way** in our nature and our actions.

The Bible defines sin as disobedience to God. This is by *transgression* (breaking His laws) or by *omission* (failing to keep them).

The Bible makes it clear "***all*** *have sinned and fall short. Of the glory of God..*". Romans 3:23

God has created mankind for his **glory**

One word for 'sin' used in the New Testament means 'missing the mark' (or target) – as one might do with bow and arrow. We all fall short of the standard that God expects of His creatures. His standard is perfection.

The reason why we sin is because **by nature** we are sinners. Lions kill and eat other animals because they are lions! It is not the acts of killing and eating that makes them lions. But because they are lions **by nature**, they kill and eat other animals. So it is that we as sinners by nature commit sins. We are rebels against God!

How did this come to be? Because we are all descendants of our forefather Adam, whom God created perfect. You may need to read the account in the first few Chapters of the Bible.

God is a **holy** God. He is perfectly righteous and good. Sin, all sin, however large or small deeply offends his holiness. God is also a perfectly just God, He must therefore justly punish all who sin. In righteousness he hates sin and those who commit sin. This is why we are called *"children of wrath"*.

> *"....among whom also we all once conducted ourselves in the lusts of our flesh, fulfilling the desires of the flesh and of the mind, and were* **by nature children of wrath**, *just as the others."* Ephesians 2:3

This is the dreadful predicament in which all humanity by nature, finds itself.

Since God is holy and also a God of truth and justice, the question arises, how can he in any way overlook sin and still be reconciled to sinners? Abraham asked God the question: *"Shall not the judge of all the earth do right?"* (Genesis 18:25), well knowing that the answer must be "yes!" On the one hand God, as a just judge, must condemn those who sin against him, whilst on the other hand, God the Father from before the creation of the earth, intended to reconcile a chosen number from among humanity.

How could God *"justify the ungodly"* ? (Romans 4:5) That is to say, "How could God who is perfectly just in all his dealings, declare a guilty person innocent?

This is what in the Good News, is being proclaimed. God has made a way. He has squared the circle! He has revealed by the prophets and apostles his plan of redemption.

This is in and through his Son who is said to be *". . . the Lamb slain from the foundation of the world*!"   Revelation 13:8

Note particularly the reason Jesus gave for his coming into the world. (Referring to himself as the Son of Man), in Luke's Gospel Chapter 19 verse 10:

"For the Son of Man came to seek and to save the lost."

HYMN

Father, 'twas Thy love that knew us
* Earth's foundation long before:*
That same love to Jesus drew us
* By its sweet constraining power*
And will keep us, and will keep us,
* Safely now, and evermore,*
* Safely now, and evermore.*

Now that changeless love enfolds us,
* All its wealth on us bestows;*
While its power unchanging holds us
* In a holy calm repose.*
God and Father, God and Father,
* Unto Thee our worship flows,*
* Unto Thee our worship flows.*

God of love, our souls adore Thee!
* We would still Thy grace proclaim,*
Till we cast our crowns before Thee,
* And in glory praise Thy name;*
Praise and worship, praise and worship
* Be to God and to the Lamb!*
* Be to God and to the Lamb!*

James George Deck 1802-1884

Chapter 3

The Cross and Salvation

I have already quoted Romans 3:23 -

"For all have sinned and fall short of the glory of God."

Now I want to look with you at what may seem to be a difficult passage of Scripture, as Paul continues in his letter to spell out **how** God has "squared the circle".

This is from Chapter 3, verses 24-26.

. . . being justified freely by His grace through the redemption that is in Christ Jesus, whom God set forth as a propitiation by His blood,

through faith, to demonstrate His righteousness, because in His forbearance God had passed over the sins that were previously committed, to demonstrate at the present time His righteousness, that He might be just and the justifier of the one who has faith in Jesus.

Let's take it bit by bit.

1. *being justified freely by his grace*

From this and other passages in the New Testament, we get the important doctrine [ix] of **'Justification by faith'.**

To be justified means that a person is reckoned to be just, or right, especially in the eyes of the law. So that we are being told that those who have broken God's laws (sinners) , who are being saved, are accounted righteous. It is as if a criminal who has committed murder is pronounced innocent in a court of law. How can God, who is a just judge do this?

2. *by His grace..*

It is by God's GRACE. That means the sinner is accounted righteous by God **entirely** through His unmerited, undeserved favour.

3. *through faith..*

God, by the Holy Spirit freely grants the gift of saving faith to a sinner.

"For by grace you have been saved through faith. And this is not your own doing; it is the gift of God, not a result of works, so that no one may boast." Ephesians 2:8-9 (ESV)

So it is not in response to our good works – our (supposed) good deeds or efforts to please God with religious observances, but through grace **alone.**

4. *Through the redemption that is in Christ Jesus...*

He who was and is the eternal Son of God, came down from heaven and took human nature. He was born of the Virgin Mary.

He was named 'Jesus' because he came "*to save His people from their sins".* Matthew 1:21

He came to save all those who were given to him by the Father before the world was made.

"*even as he chose us in him before the foundation of the world, that we should be holy and blameless before him. In love he predestined us for adoption as sons through Jesus Christ, according to the purpose of his will, to the praise of his glorious grace, with which he has blessed us in the Beloved.*

In him we have redemption through his blood, the forgiveness of our trespasses, according to the riches of his grace, which he lavished upon us, in all wisdom and insight". Ephesians 1:4-8

Again, in this passage Paul refers to the **redemption.** This word is frequently used in the Bible to echo the thought of 'paying a price to buy a slave out of slavery'. In the Old Testament, in the book of Exodus we read of how God redeemed from slavery in Egypt, those who were to form the nation of Israel.

"Let the redeemed of the LORD say so, Whom He has redeemed from the hand of the enemy, " Psalm 107:2

Jesus came to pay the price of all the sins of **all who would believe** in Him. Christ is their Redeemer. He came to redeem his people from slavery to sin.

Here we are introduced to the doctrine of 'Substitutionary Atonement'.

This is how God in His great plan of redemption, "squares the circle". Because Christ came and lived a perfect life – without sin, He was able to present himself to the Father as a perfect sacrifice, paying the penalty for all the sins of all the elect.

This he did in suffering and dying on the cross **in their place**, as their substitute. He made atonement, for their sins.

Continuing with Paul's Statement in Romans 3:

5. *whom God set forth as a propitiation by His blood...*

The word 'propitiation' is an important word in the Bible and it refers to the 'turning away of someone's anger'. Here it means the turning away of the wrath of God.

6. *that He might be just and the justifier of the one who has faith in Jesus.*

God accepts the **shed blood** of his Son, which represents his life outpoured. God's righteous wrath against sin is appeased. He is righteous and just in justifying sinners for whom his Son died.

(Read the accounts of the suffering and death of Christ on the cross, towards the end of each of the Four Gospels.)

Paul in 2 Corinthians 5:21 referring to the substitutionary sacrificial death of Christ says:

"For He made Him who knew no sin to be sin for us, that we might become the righteousness of God in Him."

God the Father **imputed** – reckoned or accounted – all the sins of his elect to be put on Christ, so that His righteousness could be **imputed** to them. Thus God is seen to be righteous in so doing.

(See also 1 Peter 2:24)

7. *who has faith in Jesus.*

We see again the doctrine that heralded the Reformation when Martin Luther in the sixteenth century, re-discovered from the Scriptures the doctrine of 'Justification by Faith alone'. That we are accounted righteous by God, not through our supposed 'good' works', but by faith alone.

There are many who recite the so-called Apostles Creed declaring that they believe that Jesus was incarnate. That he died on the cross and rose again on the third day. But that is not the same as having faith IN HIM. That is to say, believing personally in the death of Christ on the cross, as their substitute. That one's salvation is by grace alone, through God-given faith alone.

It is possible to be very 'Religious', yet not to know what it is to have saving faith in Christ. Sadly, there are many who call themselves 'Christians' who do not know what it is to be born again.

In the next Chapter we look in more detail at this and at what we might call 'The practical outworking' of redemption in the lives of each sinner who is "drawn to Christ".

(See John 6:65)

HYMN

"Tis not by works of righteousness
Which our own hands have done,
But we are saved by sovereign grace,
Abounding through the Son.

'Tis from the mercy of our God
That all out hopes begin;
'Tis by the water and the blood
That we are washed from sin.

'Tis through the purchase of his death
Who hung upon the tree,
The Spirit is sent down to breathe
On such dry bones as we.

Raised from the dead, we live again;
And justified by grace
We shall appear in glory too.
And see our Father's face.

Isaac Watts, 1674-1748

Chapter 4

The Way of Salvation

"Jesus said to him, "I am the way, the truth, and the life. No one comes to the Father except through Me." " John's Gospel 14:6

This statement of Jesus recorded in John's Gospel clearly tell us that there is only ONE way of salvation. It is through and in the person of Christ himself. There is no other way to eternal life. It is only through the redeeming sacrifice of Christ alone. How is that redemption effected or applied? Only in Christ.

"And there is salvation in no one else, for there is no other name under heaven given among men by which we must be saved." Acts 4:12

The next question is, "**How** do we come to be IN Christ?" It begins with the Word of Life – the Gospel – the Good News of salvation coming to 'dead' sinners. Just as God created the universe by His spoken word (see the first chapter of the Bible):

Then God said, "Let there be light"; and there was light." Genesis 1:3

- So he **re-creates** by His word spoken to the sinner. It is by the Holy Spirit through the word of life that sinners are regenerated – that is, "born again".

How can a Man be Born Again?

Jesus was asked this question by a ruler and teacher of the Jews, called Nicodemus. I suggest you read the account in John's Gospel, Chapter 3, verses 1-21.

From this account we learn that it is essential for any individual to be born again, if he or she is to **see o**r to **enter** the Kingdom of God – the realm in which God lives and rules. To fail to

40

enter that kingdom means that one remains in the kingdom of darkness and of Satan (Colossians 1:13 Ephesians 2: 1-3)

We also learn from the scriptures that until the new birth takes place, one is spiritually dead. (Ephesians 2:1,5 Colossians 2:13) By natural birth we are made up of body and soul. Our soul consists of our mind, emotions (or affections) and wills. Through our bodies we communicate with the world and with our souls we communicate with our bodies. But until we are given new spirits we are unable to communicate with God. (1 Corinthians 2:14).

However in the New Covenant in Jesus' blood, we are promised a new heart and a new spirit. (Ezekiel 11:19 Jeremiah 31-37) With our new – born again – spirit we can know and communicate with God.

Adam, in the garden of Eden was told by God that in the day that he ate the fruit of the forbidden tree, he would surely die. (Genesis 2: 17) but we note that his soul and body continued to live. It was his **spirit** that died. He no longer was in fellowship with God. It is with the fallen nature of Adam that we are born into this world.

Jesus told Nicodemus, "That which is born of the flesh is flesh and that which is born of the Spirit is spirit. " (John 3:7) So spiritual birth is needed.

Working Out God's Plan of Redemption

As we have shown, God's whole plan to redeem men and women from their lost spiritual state, is through the finished (complete) work of Jesus on the cross. Through the death, burial and resurrection of Jesus – being spiritually immersed (baptised)[x] into Him – we are given this new nature.

This is what the gospel – the good news – is about. Note again what Paul wrote in Ephesians 2:8 and 9

"For by grace you have been saved through faith, and that not of yourselves it is the gift of God, not of works, lest anyone should boast."

We emphasise once again, that salvation from sin and death and hell is by **grace** – that is by God's unmerited favour, which means we cannot save ourselves by our good deeds, religious rites or practices.

One example of a person being born again and coming to faith in Christ is the Philippian jailer in Acts Chapter 16. He asked, " What must I do to be saved ?." Paul's answer was that he simply needed to " *Believe on the Lord Jesus Christ*".

When the Holy Spirit comes to someone through the preaching or sharing of the gospel, they are given a new heart. From their new heart they will **repent** of their sins and believe in Jesus that He died for them personally. They received Him as their Lord and Saviour. They have been born again !

To 'repent' means to turn from our sins and all that we know to be wrong in our lives. In sorrow for all the ways in which we have grieved God -breaking his Commands and falling short of all that gives him the glory. We submit to the **Lordship** of Christ and seek his grace and power to live lives of holiness.

Saving Faith

The faith that comes through our new heart, which is evidence of true salvation, will always be 'repentant' faith. Repentance and faith are like the two sides of the same coin. It is true that we are saved by faith alone. But that faith itself is never alone. It bears fruit, as James shows in his Letter. We receive Jesus not only as our Saviour and Redeemer, but also as our Lord and King! He is now our Master and Teacher. We become his disciples.[xi]

As we shall note later, that as a new disciple he or she will need to be baptised (immersed) in water to show that they have died to an old life and risen to a new one. They will need to feed on the Word of God in the Bible in order to grow. This will be through joining in fellowship with other Christians. Prayer will become an important part of their lives.

HYMN

'Tis not that I did choose Thee
For, Lord, that could not be;
This heart would still refuse Thee
Had Thou not chosen me.

Thou from the sin that stained me
Hast cleansed and set me free;
Of old Thou didst ordain me,
That I should live to Thee.

'Twas sovereign mercy called me,
And taught my opening mind;
The world had else enthralled me,
To heavenly glories blind.

My heart owns none above Thee;
For Thy rich grace I thirst;
This knowing, if I love Thee,
Thou must have loved me first!

Josiah Conder. 1789-1855

Chapter 5

The Great Commission

"And Jesus came and spoke to them, saying, "All authority has been given to Me in heaven and on earth.

Go therefore and make disciples of all the nations, baptising them in the name of the Father and of the Son and of the Holy Spirit, teaching them to observe all things that I have commanded you; and lo, I am with you always, even to the end of the age." Amen."
Matthew 28:18-20

This command by Jesus to the first disciples is known as "The Great Commission". It is the 'marching orders' to his disciples in every age, until he comes again.

We notice four important things in this final command.

1. *Go therefore....* As disciples of Jesus, we are commanded to GO. We are not to passively wait for sinners to **Come** to hear the gospel. But we are to take it to sinners in every possible place.

2. *Make disciples....* Every true disciple is called to make further disciples. There is a particular calling for 'Evangelists' (Ephesians 411). But every believer, however new in the faith, is called to share that faith with others.

3. *Baptising them....* As soon as someone becomes a disciple through faith in Christ, he or she is commanded to be baptised in water. The word 'baptise' is simply the New Testament Greek word for 'immerse'. You will find this numerous times in the Acts of the Apostles. Each time we read of someone being converted, they are immediately baptised in water. Water baptism does not save anyone. It is an outward testimony to having been spiritually immersed into Christ. (1Cor. 12:13). We have died to an old life,

been buried, and raised to this new life in Christ.

4. *Teach them to observe all....* New disciples need mentoring. They need to be taught **everything** Christ has taught us.

Disciples Who Make Disciples

As we read the account of the beginning of the Church of Jesus Christ in the Acts of the Apostles, we might be amazed at the tremendous expansion of the number of believers in such a short period of time.

There are two things to notice about this. Firstly, we read of the power of the Holy Spirit being poured out in those days. Secondly, we might notice **how** the gospel spread.

The outpouring of the Holy Spirit is according to the sovereign gifting and timing of God. But this in turn, is not unrelated to the prayers of God's people.

We next note that God's people, under the New Covenant in the blood of Jesus, are very rarely called 'Christians'. But many times they are called 'Disciples'.

What does it mean to be a disciple of Jesus? The word 'disciple' is a translation of a word that means a 'learner'.

Jesus was addressed as Rabbi by his followers. In that time there were various 'Rabbis' or 'Teachers' among the Jews. Some, like Jesus were itinerant Teachers who went from place to place teaching. Their disciples – learners or students, accompanied their Teacher as he travelled about. When Jesus called to the first disciples saying, "Follow me!", this is what he was calling them to do.

Jesus spent most of his time with his disciples, teaching and training them to become disciple-makers themselves. Before he returned to heaven, he gave them this last command, which we call the Great Commission.

This was meant to be continued in every age until all nations have heard the gospel and Jesus returns in glory.

Sadly, for centuries, believers have not been taught or expected to be disciples. Instead, they have been kept as 'children' under their teachers. But one of the main reasons the gospel spread so rapidly in the first years of the Church, was because believers were taught to become disciples who make disciples.

Every disciple, however new, is called by Christ to make further disciples, teaching them everything they have themselves been taught.

Many feel inadequate in this task, yet if their new found faith in Christ is real, they will be bursting to tell others. But our spiritual enemy (Satan), would want to rob us of this desire by fear – including the fear that we do not know how to share saving faith. So, let's set out in the essentials of the Gospel, that every new believer might share.

Start with prayer. Ask the Father for the help of the Holy Spirit, in Jesus' name.

Go on with prayer. *"Pray without ceasing."*

Read and study the Bible. Memorise some passages (texts) that show the Way of salvation, such as those already quoted.

So where to begin?

Note how Jesus dialogued with individuals, encouraging questions. Read the account of his conversations with Nicodemus, the Samaritan woman at the well, also with those who opposed him

John 3:9, John 4:7, Mark 2:7 etc..

There is no 'set way' to present the gospel to others. We must be open to the leading of the Holy Spirit. However, as we have shown, there is an essential content to the Good News. Paul reminds the Corinthians of this content in First Corinthians 15: 1-4

"Moreover, brethren, I declare to you the gospel which I preached to you, which also you received and in which you stand, by which also you are saved, if you hold fast that word which I preached to you—unless you believed in vain.

For I delivered to you first of all that which I also received: that Christ died for our sins according to the Scriptures, and that He was buried, and that He rose again the third day according to the Scriptures,"

Any presentation of the Gospel will centre around the death, burial and resurrection of Jesus in accordance with what was prophesied about him in the Old Testament scriptures.

New disciples need to be reminded of two things that might inhibit them from sharing the Gospel with others.

The first is that our spiritual enemy, Satan, hates the gospel being presented and will attempt to dissuade you from doing so. So make sure you are wearing the armour of God. (Ephesians 6:14-18)   Go on the offensive with the *"sword of the Spirit, which is the Word of God".*

The second is that you need to familiarise yourself with Scriptures you can point to. Marking them in your Bibles may prove useful.

But note carefully, that there is no 'magic bullet' plan. With every person, the Holy Spirit must guide us in what and when we speak to them of the gospel. Until the Holy Spirit 'turns the light on' in a person's heart – they will remain in darkness no matter what preaching they may hear or Scriptures they read!

A Further Note of Caution

Some use a 'plan' to present the gospel and then press their hearers to recite a "sinners prayer". This may be attempting something that only the Holy Spirit can do. (John 16:80

We are commissioned to tell the Good News. Only the Holy Spirit can convict of sin, regenerate and produce true conversion.

HYMN

Himself He could not save,
He on the cross must die,
Or mercy could not come
To ruined sinners nigh;
Yes, Christ, the Son of God, must bleed
That sinners might from sin be freed.

Himself He could not save,
For justice must be done;
Our sins' full weight must fall
Upon the sinless One;
For nothing less could God accept
In payment of that fearful debt.

Himself He could not save,
For He the Surety stood
For all who now rely
Upon His precious blood;
He bore the penalty of guilt
When on the cross His blood was spilt.

Himself He could not save,
Love's stream too deeply flowed,
In love Himself He gave,
To pay the debt we owed.
Obedience to His Father's will,
And love to Him did all fulfil.

Albert Midlane   1825-1909

Chapter 6

False 'Gospels' & Advice to New Believers

False Gospels

The apostle Paul, writing in his Letter to the Galatians, warns them of the danger of "false gospels", which are not 'gospels' at all! He has the strongest condemnation for those who preach them, using the word 'anathema', cursing them to hell!

"there are some who trouble you and want to pervert the gospel of Christ. But even if we, or an angel from heaven, preach any other gospel to you than what we have preached to you, let him be accursed." Galatians 1:7,8

The reason he felt so strongly about this was because false gospels may persuade hearers that they are in the way of salvation, when in fact, they are on their way to condemnation!

Jesus, in the "Sermon on the Mount" utters a fearful warning: *"Many will say to Me in that day, 'Lord, Lord, have we not prophesied in Your name, cast out demons in Your name, and done many wonders in Your name?' And then I will declare to them, '**I never knew you**; depart from Me..."* (Matthew 7: 21-23)

False 'gospels' and false gospel preachers abound in our day. Those who do not accept the authority of the Bible – often referred to as 'liberals' – they will preach about 'God loving the world' and exhort men to live moral lives, but the gospel is absent.

There are four particular false 'gospels' that are prevalent today that may deceive those who see themselves as 'evangelicals'.

1. The first is the one Paul wrote to the Galatians about. It is a 'Hybrid' gospel. That

is, one that mixes something with grace. In this case it is mixing Law with grace. The false preachers were trying to get believers to keep some parts of the Law of Moses for salvation. Today, believers are persuaded, although they are "justified by grace alone`", they need to keep the Ten Commandments in order to become holy. This produces a form of 'legalism'. The true gospel of grace alone, brings salvation and conversion to believers. So now, from their new hearts, they desire to keep **all** God's commands that relate to them under the New Covenant, as found in the Scriptures of the New Testament.

2. The second false 'gospel' is not new, but named after s Scottish preacher, Robert Sandeman (1718-1781). His followers taught that **simple agreement** with the historical **facts** – that Jesus became man, died on the cross and rose again, was all that was needed to be saved.

People may be persuaded of the historical truths, and encouraged to recite them in the

'Creeds'. This, the 'natural man' (1 Corinthians 2:14) can do, but it is not evidence of regeneration and true salvation.

3.   The third false 'gospel' is known as "The Prosperity Gospel". This is widely preached on U.S. television channels by 'tele-evangelists'. It is also preached by some "charismatic" and "Pentecostal" sources.

In essence what they preach is that if you accept Jesus into your life (or heart), provided you have faith to believe it, you will prosper **materially** as well as spiritually. You will be kept free from sickness and diseases.

Their message is usually bound up with the so-called 'Faith Movement'. What this really amounts to is faith in your own faith. If you run into debt or are sick, it is because you do not have enough faith in God as your provider and Jesus as your healer.

This is put forward by taking verses and promises in Scripture out of context. Any study of the warnings of Jesus and the

60

apostles about "cross-bearing" or suffering for the gospel's sake by Paul and Peter will demonstrate the false content of this 'gospel'. Also the wrong application of promises given to Israel under the Old Covenant, as though they are promises given to all believers under the New Covenant.

"Your prosperity will be multiplied back to you in proportion to your giving." (Especially, of course, in your giving to the preacher or his organisation!)

4. The fourth most widespread false 'gospel' is known as "Easy-believism".

Those who preach it will say that they believe in salvation by grace alone. But they teach that "God loves everyone" and 'Christ died for everyone'. Therefore, they suggest, all that anyone needs to do to "get themselves saved" is to take these three steps:

1 Say you are sorry to God for your sins.

2. Ask His forgiveness, and

3. Receive Christ as your Saviour in prayer - 'inviting Jesus into you heart'.

Once you have done this, they say, you can be assured that you are saved. They may quote Romans 10;9 (out of context) to confirm it.

I trust the reader will understand why this is labelled an "easy-believism" gospel.

That some have come to salvation through such a presentation, I do not doubt. But this is not the way Jesus or the first apostles presented the gospel.

What we can do, is pray for those we witness to. We can exhort the lost to repent and believe, well aware that they cannot and will not do so until the Word of Life is given to produce spiritual life in them. Even as Ezekiel was commanded to preach to dry dead bones that they might live. Or as Jesus spoke the word of life to Lazarus who was dead in the tomb for four days. (Read Ezekiel Chapter 37 & John's Gospel Chapter 11)

It is essential that our aim is **not** to try and make 'converts', but to present the one true Gospel of grace. If, as a result there are converts, we are to teach them discipleship.

Advice to New Believers

The following advice may be given to help new believers:

Just as a new-born baby grows physically, in a similar way we grow spiritually, by seeking the help of the Holy Spirit in the following ways:

Reading the Bible

Starting with the Gospel of John, read a section each day. "*As new-born babes, desire the sincere milk of the Word (of God), that you may grow thereby*" (1 Peter 2:2).

See how what you read and think about, might apply to you today.

Pray

Spend time each day talking with God. *"Be anxious for nothing; but in everything by prayer and supplication with thanksgiving let your requests be made known unto God"* (Philippians 4:6).

Worship

Become active in a church that honours Jesus Christ, reaches out with a true gospel, and teaches you the Bible.

It may be that there is no such church in your area, if so, it may be that you are being called to begin one!

"God is a Spirit: and they that worship Him must worship Him in spirit and truth" (John 4:24).

Fellowship

If possible, meet with other Christians who will help you grow in faith. *"That which we have seen and heard declare we unto you, that you also may have fellowship with us: and truly our fellowship is with the Father, and with His Son Jesus Christ*" (1 John 1:3).

Each believer is given one or more particular gift. Seek to share in mutual "body-ministry". (See 1 Corinthians 12.)

Witness

Tell others what Jesus Christ means to you! "*But you shall receive power, after that the Holy Ghost is come upon you: and you shall be witnesses unto Me . . .*" (Acts 1:8).

Doing all these things will not make you a Disciple, but if you are a disciple you will find them helpful as you follow the Master and learn from Him.

BE BAPTISED AND GO, MAKE DISCIPLES!

HYMN

O for a thousand tongues to sing
my great Redeemer's praise,
the glories of my God and King,
the triumphs of his grace!

My gracious Master and my God,
assist me to proclaim,
to spread thro' all the earth abroad
the honors of your name.

Jesus! the name that charms our fears,
that bids our sorrows cease,
'tis music in the sinner's ears,
'tis life and health and peace.

He breaks the power of cancelled sin,
he sets the prisoner free;
his blood can make the foulest clean;
his blood availed for me.

To God all glory, praise, and love
be now and ever given
by saints below and saints above,
the Church in earth and heaven.

Chares Wesley 1707-88

Chapter 7

Conclusion

By way of conclusion, let me remind you of the aims of the book, set out in the Introduction.

1. The first aim was to show the need of salvation. We trust that this is clearly recognised.

2. The second aim was to show that salvation is through the gospel being shared.

3. The third aim was to show that there is only ONE true Gospel but numerous false ones. My hope is that the distinction can clearly be made.

4. The fourth aim was to encourage all who may already call themselves 'Christians' to examine themselves to see whether they are

truly in the Way of Salvation. - Asking two key questions:

(a) For whom did Christ die?

(b) What is your part in getting saved?

We trust you have found clear answers to these two questions.

Two further questions:

1.Are you among those for whom Christ died?

2.Have you been saved ENTIRELY by GRACE ALONE – through FAITH ALONE in the blood of Christ ALONE?

My prayer is that you will joyfully answer "Yes" to both. The Gospel of Grace, is the only gospel that gives ALL the glory to God and is the ONE TRUE GOSPEL.

5. My fifth aim was to encourage ALL believers to take their part in response to the 'Great Commission'- proclaim **this Gospel** in and to ALL the world!

HYMN

Amazing grace! How sweet the sound
That saved a wretch like me!
I once was lost, but now am found;
Was blind, but now I see.

'Twas grace that taught my heart to fear,
And grace my fears relieved;
How precious did that grace appear
The hour I first believed.

Through many dangers, toils and snares,
I have already come;
'Tis grace hath brought me safe thus far,
And grace will lead me home.

The Lord has promised good to me,
His word my hope secures;
He will my shield and portion be,
As long as life endures.

Yea, when this flesh and heart shall fail,
And mortal life shall cease,
I shall possess, within the veil,
A life of joy and peace.

The world shall soon dissolve like snow,
The sun refuse to shine;
But God, who called me here below,
Shall be forever mine.

When we've been there ten thousand years,
Bright shining as the sun,
We've no less days to sing God's praise
Than when we'd first begun. - John Newton 1779

Appendix A

Recommended Bible Versions:

New King James Version (NKJV)

New American Standard version (NASB)

English Standard Version (ESV)

New International Version (NIV) This version is in easier English, using "thought for thought" translation, rather than "word for word".

The Author

Fred Serjeant has been married to Mary for 60 years and they have three sons, six grandchildren and have one great grandson. Fred has been in pastoral and evangelistic ministry for 65 years, He is the author of six other books published through Amazon:

"Understanding the New Covenant" A Simple Introduction to New Covenant Theology

"Make Disciples!". Making Disciples who make Disciples – A Discipleship Manual.

"12 Steps Out – A manual for Freedom from Addiction"

"Living in the New Covenant" Enjoying the freedom believers have been granted in Christ.

"The Twelve Pillars of the Christian Faith" A Manual of Basic Christian Doctrines for new believers and for those whose doctrine is "woolly".

"Arminianism and the Doctrines of Grace" A comparison of the two main views of the way of salvation

All available in Paperback and most also in Kindle versions at amazon.co.uk or amazon.com

Note from the Author:

If you have any questions about the teaching in this book which you would like to ask me (the author), please go to my website at:

www.simplechurch.org.uk

_Facebook:

Frederick Serjeant

Twitter:

@FredSerjeant

or email me at

 f.serjeant@gmail.com

END NOTES

---

[i] The word GRACE means "Gods unmerited favour." (PLEASE TAKE NOTE OF ALL THE END NOTES)

[ii] Compare 2 Corinthians 2:17

[iii] From this point on we intend to include **both genders** when we say he, him etc..

[iv] 'Christ' is not a surname but a title. It is the English form of the Greek word *Christos* – the Hebrew being *Messiah* –or Anointed One

[v] As we shall see later, 'repentance refers to 'turning from our sins' and 'believing' refers to having faith in Christ and what he has done.

[vi] The word **'Apostle'** means Special Messenger – One appointed and sent out with a message.

[vii] The word **'saints'** is used in the Bible to refer to **all t**rue Christians – not to special **super ones!**

[viii] 'Greek" here means all non-Jews, i.e. Gentiles

[ix] Don't be put off by the word 'doctrine'! It simply means important teaching.

79

[x] We are not referring to baptism (immersion) in water here.

[xi] 'Disciple' – one who is a 'learner' – following a Teacher.

THE END

41673071R00047

Printed in Poland
by Amazon Fulfillment
Poland Sp. z o.o., Wrocław